PRISONS AND PUNISHMENT

Graham Rickard

The Bookwright Press
New York · 1987

Topics

The Age of Dinosaurs
Airports
Ancient Peoples
Archaeology
Bridges
Castles
Costumes and Clothes
Earthquakes and Volcanoes
Energy
Fairs and Circuses
Farm Animals
Ghosts and the Supernatural
Great Disasters .
Helicopters
Houses and Homes

Inventions
Jungles
Maps and Globes
Money
Musical Instruments
Peoples of the World
Photography
Pollution and Conservation
Prisons and Punishment
Robots
Spacecraft
Television
Trees of the World
Under the Ground
Zoos

All the words that appear
in **bold** are explained in the
glossary on page 30.

Phototypeset by
Kalligraphics Ltd, Redhill, Surrey
Printed in
Belgium by
Casterman S.A.

First published in the
United States in 1987 by
The Bookwright Press
New York, NY 10016

First published in 1987 by
Wayland (Publishers) Ltd
61 Western Road, Hove
East Sussex BN3 1JD, England

© Copyright 1987 Wayland (Publishers) Ltd

ISBN 0–531–18147–2
Library of Congress Catalog Card Number: 86–73118

Contents

Crime and Punishment

From the earliest times to the present day, humankind has always liked to live in groups. People don't always agree with each other, so every society, from the smallest tribe to the largest nation, has its own system of laws and rules to protect the lives and property of its members. Some people are given

A chained prisoner is brought to trial in nineteenth-century China.

Judge Roy Bean acted as both judge and jury from his saloon-courthouse in Texas. This picture was taken around 1900.

the power to make sure that laws are not broken, by punishing anyone who disobeys the rules.

You probably belong to several societies, each with its own set of rules, including your family, your school and your country. If you misbehave at home, your parents may punish you, while it is the school principal who enforces the rules of your school. If you break the laws of your country, you may be tried by a **magistrate** or **judge**.

There are many different types of punishment, and every society in every age has had its own way of dealing with criminals. What is normal behavior in some societies

In the nineteenth century many thousands of convicted people were transported from Britain to Australia. Some early convicts in Tasmania are shown here.

A new arrival at Newgate Prison in London in the early nineteenth century.

may be strictly punished in others; in some Islamic countries, for example, people are sometimes whipped for drinking alcohol, and thieves may still have their hands cut off.

Throughout most of history, the main forms of punishment have been death by execution (**capital punishment**), whipping and other forms of **corporal punishment**, being banished from society or having to pay a fine. It is only quite recently that criminals have been punished by being locked up in a prison, away from their homes, families and friends.

Ideas about punishment have changed over the years, and society is now much kinder to criminals than it used to be. In the past, society demanded "an eye for an eye, and a tooth for a tooth," and used harsh punishments to take its revenge on criminals, making them pay their "debt" to society. Execution and **floggings** were carried out in public, in the belief that strict punishment would stop other people from committing similar crimes. But there is little evidence that punishments have any effect on the amount of crime in society, and criminals often commit the same **offense** time after time. Because of this, people's views are changing, and punishments are now often meant to help criminals change their ideas about crime and become accepted into society, rather than to cut them off from other people.

Two methods of corporal punishment: the treadmill (top) and the cat-o'-nine-tails (bottom).

Jews being transported to a concentration camp.

People who have committed no crime are still sometimes punished or imprisoned for their beliefs or religion. This happened in World War II, when millions of Jews were rounded up in Europe and **tortured** and killed in **concentration camps** by Hitler's **Nazis**. Even in times of war, there are international rules intended to prevent these terrible "war crimes," and prisoners-of-war throughout the world are protected by the rules of the **Geneva Convention**.

Punishments through the Ages

Over the centuries, people have shown imagination and much cruelty in thinking up painful punishments for their fellow human beings who have broken the law. In the past, the punishment was supposed to fit the crime, but wrongdoers who had committed only minor offenses were often treated savagely, as society took its terrible revenge in the name of "justice."

The severest punishment of all is the death sentence, which was once used for a wide variety of crimes. Each society has had its own methods of legal execution, many of them slow and painful. In Biblical times, criminals were often stoned to death, while the Romans crucified thieves on a wooden cross.

The Romans often crucified people they thought to be criminals. This picture shows Jesus's crucifixion.

In the Middle Ages, offenders were sometimes crushed to death, either on a large wheel or by heavy weights on their chests.

In more recent times, the English **gallows**, the French **guillotine** and the American **electric chair** have been traditional punishments for murderers. Strangulation,

An early electric chair in the United States.

beheading, drowning, gassing, lethal injections and shooting by firing squad have all been used as legal methods of execution. Capital punishment is now thought by many people to be too severe, and has been totally abolished by many Western countries. But several states in the United States have begun using the death penalty again, and many people in Europe would like to see terrorists executed.

The guillotine was the favored method of capital punishment in France. This picture shows Louis XVI's execution by guillotine in 1793.

Corporal punishment causes physical pain to the offender, and was once commonly used for minor offenses. Some of these punishments, such as the cutting off of hands and feet, would be very brutal by modern standards. People guilty of **blasphemy** had their tongues cut out, while thieves were branded on the face with a red-hot iron. Such mutilations and public floggings often led to a slow death through loss of blood or infection of the wounds, and were common in Europe until the seventeenth century. Almost every

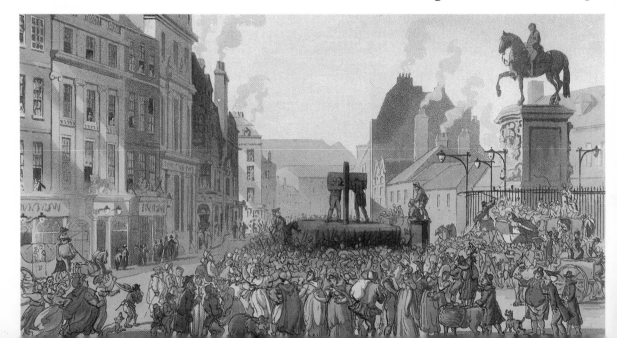

The pillory at London's Charing Cross in 1809.

town also had its **pillory** or **stocks**, into which drunkards and **vagrants** were locked, to be ridiculed and pelted with rubbish by passing citizens. Fortunately, these punishments have now been abolished in most countries, although physical torture is still sometimes used to get information from prisoners.

The payment of fines as a punishment has a long history, and is widely used today for many offenses. The amount of money that the criminal has to pay to the state depends not only on the seriousness of the offense, but also on how much the offender can afford to pay. Those who have little money can pay their fines in **installments**, and are usually fined less than a wealthy person who has committed the same offense. The money that is collected in fines helps to pay for the police force and the law courts.

A New York policeman arresting a drunk in the 1890s. A fine or short prison sentence was the usual punishment for such an offense.

Prisons

Prisoners have always been locked up in **jails** and **dungeons**, but until fairly recently such places were only used to hold people awaiting trial, punishment or execution. Taking away people's freedom by locking them up in secure cells, has been used as a punishment only since the eighteenth century, when there was a great reduction in the use of the death penalty.

An old village lockup in Hertfordshire, England. Prisoners were kept here for short periods while they were awaiting trial.

This painting of a prison scene by Goya shows how gloomy prisons were in the early nineteenth century.

In the sixteenth century minor criminals were sent to "houses of correction." A famous house of correction in England was Bridewell. Similar institutions were set up in the American Colonies.

Early prisons were dark, damp and filthy, and prisoners were often treated very badly. Men, women and children were thrown together in one room. They were often chained to the wall, with no fresh

The entrance to Newgate Prison in London. The first jail to be built at Newgate dates from the twelfth century but a new one was built in 1672.

air, clean water or bathrooms. Jailers were often cruel and, because they received no wages, made their prisoners pay for the "privilege" of food and straw bedding. It is not surprising that hundreds of prisoners died in the many epidemics of "jail-fever" (usually **typhoid**) that occurred throughout the prisons of Europe.

These terrible conditions were eventually improved by the ideas of the great English prison reformer John Howard, who was the High Sheriff of Bedfordshire in the late eighteenth century. Horrified by the prisons of England and Europe, he suggested that jail-keepers should be paid a regular wage by the state, and that prisoners should be kept in separate cells and given some useful work to do.

In the United States, too, fines and imprisonment began to replace execution as the major forms of punishment. By 1794, murder was the only **capital offense** remaining in the state of Pennsylvania.

Howard's ideas were taken up by later reformers in both Europe and the United States. A "model prison" was built in 1825 in Auburn, New York. In 1842 Pentonville, the first of fifty-four **model prisons**, was built in London. Conditions were still harsh, and prisoners had to do

John Howard, the great prison reformer, is shown here trying to deal with a prison riot.

Prisoners exercising at the Ohio Penitentiary, in Columbus, Ohio, in about 1847.

long hours of "hard labor," building roads, canals and even prisons. But prison life became bearable for the first time.

*A **chain gang** at work in Georgia, in the 1930s.*

Prison Life Today

In modern prisons, new prisoners have to take off their clothes and hand in all their possessions, before being given a medical checkup and a prison uniform. The guards show them to their cells, where they will spend nearly all of their time while in prison.

Most prisons now try to reform rather than punish their **inmates**, and in many prisons there are opportunities to study or train for a career in the outside world. Prisons have their own **chaplains**, **psychiatrists** and doctors to look after the inmates. Prison libraries and gyms are usually well used, and prisoners can join their own sports teams. Prisoners who are violent or mentally ill are put into special **high-security prisons**, while open prisons are more relaxed about security, because

A prison counselor talking to inmates of the Manila City Jail in the Philippines.

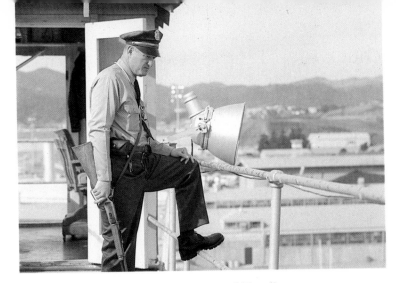

An armed prison guard at the high-security San Quentin Prison in California.

In a modern prison inmates can attend courses and take examinations, which may help them get a job when they leave prison.

their inmates are not likely to try to escape.

Each prison is run by a **warden**, who is responsible for organizing the work of the guards and other staff, and overseeing the prisoners. It is a difficult job because even in a modern prison, the inmates resent the loss of their freedom and privacy. The prison warden's task is often made even more difficult by the problems of overcrowding and out-of-date buildings.

A prisoner's day follows a strict routine, and life is governed by rules and regulations.

The prison gates are unlocked early in the morning, and guards check their keys as they arrive for the day shift. When the prisoners are dressed, their cells are unlocked, and, if the cell has no toilet, they line up to empty and wash their chamber-pots. This is known as "slopping out." Supervised by the guards, the prisoners then have breakfast, either in their cells or in the prison cafeteria.

After breakfast, the prison chaplain holds a service in the chapel for any prisoners who want to attend, and this is followed by an exercise period in an enclosed yard. Regular exercise is very important for prisoners, who spend most of their time in small cells. Many prisoners also use the prison gym to keep fit.

Prison vans are on hand to take **remand** prisoners to court appearances, or to transfer them to other prisons.

Education is an important way of

Prisoners having their meal in a prison cafeteria.

An inmate carefully tends the prison garden.

beating boredom, and prisoners can use the library and attend courses in crafts, handiwork, and other useful subjects, which may make it easier for them to find work when they are released.

Prisoners attending a history lesson.

Working parties start work early in the morning. Besides doing all the cleaning and cooking duties in the prison, inmates can earn a little money by working in the prison factories. Trusted prisoners may even work outside the prison, on farms, roadworks and building projects.

At lunchtime, prisoners are locked in their cells again while they eat their meal and wait for the afternoon visiting session. There is a visitors' room where inmates can meet their families and friends, and these visits are an important high spot in a prisoner's life. Visitors can bring presents of food, drink and cigarettes, but packages are all carefully searched by the prison staff, in case they contain alcohol, drugs or weapons. Just in case these things do get into the prison, all cells are regularly searched as well.

After the evening meal, prisoners can socialize in the period

In the prison workshop, inmates can learn skills such as bricklaying and carpentry.

sometimes known as "association." In this free time, they can play games, watch television or just talk together, before being locked up for the night.

The gray granite stone of Dartmoor Prison in Devon, England.

New Ideas in Punishment

Over the last fifty years, there have been many changes in the treatment of those who break the law. Most offenders are now merely fined, and prison sentences and other punishments are used in an attempt to reform the criminal's character. Women have separate prisons, while young offenders are sent to special **detention** centers to await trail. If convicted, young offenders may be sent to juvenile institutions such as **reformatories** or to stricter centers, where they

An inmate in a special unit for drug addicts at a prison in Baltimore, Maryland.

The island of Alcatraz in San Francisco Bay housed a federal prison until 1963.

receive "no nonsense" treatment with a high level of discipline.

But the prisons of most countries are still very overcrowded, with three prisoners often sharing a small cell designed for one person. Together with a lack of prison staff, these conditions can lead to frustration and unrest, and prison riots are easily sparked off. Prisons often have a hardening effect on criminals, by cutting them off from the rest of society and the outside world, and there have been many attempts to find alternative means of punishment.

Well-behaved prisoners are often granted **remission**, and released early from prison on **parole**, on the condition that they commit no further offenses. Open prisons, based on Scandinavian prisons of the 1920s, are run on more relaxed lines, and sometimes prisoners have to attend only on weekends. Some offenders are put on **probation**, which means that they have to see a probation officer once a week. This is often a very successful form of **sentence** for young offenders who need responsible advice and guidance.

Experimental sentences have been tried using an electronic "ball

A life sentence prisoner can spend ten or more years in a cell like this one.

Perhaps new methods of punishment will make the sending of people to prison a thing of the past.

and chain" to keep an offender under a form of house arrest. A radio transmitter is fixed to the offender's ankle, giving out a signal that tells the police if a person has moved out of the approved area.

Another experimental idea is to make the offender pay for a full apology to the community in the local newspapers, including a photograph of the offender. The shame of being recognized in the street has persuaded many offenders to move away from their areas altogether. This project is regarded as successful in places where it has been tried.

Rather than receive a prison sentence, some offenders agree to work a number of hours on a **community service** program, doing such useful jobs as decorating schools and old people's homes. Some offenders, under a compensation order, have to pay damages to the victim of their crime. Sometimes, a person who is found guilty by the courts is given a **suspended prison sentence**, which is not put into effect unless the criminal commits another offense.

Many of these modern forms of punishment are both much cheaper and more effective than locking someone away in a cell, cut off from work, family and friends. Society is beginning to realize that criminals usually need help rather than punishment, and that cruelty does not always deter crime.

Christmas decorations at Strangeways Jail, in Manchester, England.

Glossary

Blasphemy Words or actions that show disrespect for God.

Capital offense A serious crime for which death is the punishment.

Capital punishment Execution under a death sentence.

Chain gang A group of prisoners who are chained together while doing hard labor.

Chaplain A minister, priest or rabbi who works for a particular organization or institution.

Community service An alternative to prison, in which the offender works a certain number of hours on a community work program.

Concentration camp A guarded prison camp in which large numbers of people are held, often in terrible conditions.

Corporal punishment A form of punishment, such as flogging, that causes physical pain.

Detention The act of detaining or keeping someone in custody.

Dungeon A small dark cell, often found underground in castles.

Electric chair A form of execution in which an offender is strapped to a chair and then receives a lethal current of electricity.

Flogging Beating with a whip or strap.

Gallows A wooden structure supporting a rope, used for hanging offenders.

Geneva Convention An international agreement, dating from 1864, protecting the rights of prisoners-of-war.

Guillotine A French method of execution, which cuts off the victim's head with a heavy sharp blade.

High-security prison A heavily guarded prison where dangerous prisoners are sent.

Inmate A prisoner.

Installments Portions into which a fine or debt is divided to be paid over a period of time.

Jail A local, city or county prison.

Judge A person in charge of a higher court of law that deals with major crimes.

Magistrate A person in charge of a lower court that deals with minor crimes.

Model prison The name given to a new type of prison that is meant to be a "model" for later prisons.

Nazi A member of Hitler's

National Socialist German Workers' Party, which took control of Germany in 1933.

Offense A crime. Someone who commits a crime is called an **offender**.

Parole The freeing of a prisoner before his or her full sentence has been served on the condition that he or she behaves well.

Pillory A wooden framework into which offenders were locked by the neck and wrists.

Probation A method of supervising offenders out in the community.

Psychiatrist A doctor who treats people who are mentally ill rather than physically ill.

Reformatory A place where young offenders are sent for training and discipline.

Remand The holding of a prisoner who is awaiting a court appearance.

Remission The reduction or pardon of a prison sentence.

Sentence A punishment decided by a judge or magistrate in a court of law.

Stocks A wooden framework into which offenders were locked by the feet, hands or neck.

Suspended prison sentence A sentence that only comes into effect if the offender commits another crime.

Torture To cause horrible pain to someone.

Typhoid A deadly infectious disease often caused by dirty water and unhygienic conditions.

Vagrant A person with no fixed home, job or income.

Warden An official in charge of a prison.

Books to Read

The American Legal System by E. B. Fincher. Franklin Watts, 1980.

The Death Penalty: The Case of the Life VS. Death in the United States by Leonard A. Stevens. Putnam, 1978.

Guilty or Innocent by Anita Gustafson. Holt, Rhinehart & Winston, 1985.

Learning About Towers and Dungeons by Leone C. Anderson. Children Press, 1982

Prison Life In America by Anna Kosof. Franklin Watts, 1984.

Index

Picture acknowledgments
The pictures in this book were supplied by the following: The Bridgeman Library 15; E.T. Archive 4; Mary Evans 5 (bottom), 6, 7, 9, 11, 12; H.M. Prison Services Museum 20 (bottom), 21, 22 (both), 24 (top), 25; The Mansell Collection 17; Peter Newark's Western Americana 5 (top), 10, 13, 18 (both); Syndication International 29; Topham 14, 24 (bottom), 25, 26, 27; The Wayland Picture Library 8, 16, 19; Zefa 20 (top).